The
Husband Whisperer

Kathryn C. Lang

ISBN-13: 978-1492312239
ISBN-10: 1492312231

Cover images have been adapted by Kathryn C. Lang
from original photography taken by Buddy Taylor.

All Scripture references are paraphrased in the
words of the author unless otherwise noted.

Logo image developed by Lewis Screen Printing &
Monogramming for the exclusive use of Kathryn C.
Lang.

Acknowledgements

A successful marriage involves three and not just two. I want to thank my dad for teaching me to build a marriage on the foundation of Christ.

Building that marriage has required change, hard work and more than a few tears. I want to thank Keith for being willing to take the journey with me.

Thank you also to all of you who are willing to invest your time in the words that I share in the book. May all that you read inspire and encourage you the way the journey continues to inspire and encourage me.

The
Husband Whisperer

Kathryn C. Lang

*Get the eight secrets you need to have the
husband you have always wanted.*

Content

Introduction

"Get the top eight secrets for changing the heart, mind and attitude of a husband by making the changes happen in your own life."

The day I got married I refused to check my attitude and personality at the door. I would be my own woman and chart my own course. My husband would just be blessed enough to join me for the ride. My life of standing firm against authority had prepared me for the tough path I would be tredding.

I married a man with just as hard a head as I had, so you can imagine the fun and firworks of the first few years. Our long history and solid friendship were probably two of the main reasons that we survived. A desire to change and become the one we were designed to be had not yet sprouted in our hearts or minds. There are times when I am certain it may have been sheer stubbornness that managed to hold our marriage together – neither wanted to be the first to fold.

A series of events pushed me to begin a journey that has been painful, frustrating and unfair - at times. At least, those are the views from the pit. Getting to the top of each hill allowed me to see that my actions and my attitudes had been hurting and hindering all of those around me. By choosing to change I made room for our marriage to grow.

[1]

Because I chose to take the pressure off my husband I gave him the ability to begin becoming all that he could be on his OWN terms.

The journey continues each day and some days I do better than others. I try to continue to make better choices that will help me become the wife I was designed to be and help me understand just what it takes to train a husband.

"Say something nice – not because the saying will bless someone else (although it will) but because the words that you share will bless your own heart."

Secret 1

Encouragement Goes a Long Way

"As a man thinks, so is he." A man needs to hear his strengths and positives if he is going to believe in them. A man has to believe in his strengths and positives if he is going to become them.

I heard an expert in family counseling discussing how men of today are designed by society to be failures. The definition of success defined by the world centers on the ability to create or maintain extreme wealth and fame. Things that focus around character - being a provider, active father, supportive husband and a good person - are ignored or buried (or worse, scorned).

I heard a writer talking at a writer's conference and she said that I needed to define my success between me and God so that I would not leave my destiny up to the world. Experts could learn from what she had to offer that day. The world sets us up for failure, but God prepares a way of exceeding abundance for His children.

My words and my actions may not delete the expectations of the world, but they can begin to grow and nurture a new expectation in the heart and mind of my husband.

Developing a Lifestyle of Encouragement

- Remember that encouragement is a willful action. It must be a choice. That may mean sacrificing a little of self (putting down the book to listen or closing the laptop to provide the undivided attention desired).

- Practice encouragement daily. Look for opportunities to speak good, positive and uplifting things to your spouse. Make them real and in his "love" language if possible. If he does something around the house or spends time with the kids, let him know that you appreciate who he is and what he does. Hebrews 3:13 reminds us to encourage each other daily, as long as it is called today.

- Move beyond the words. Encouragement lays a foundation for lifting up others and even carrying others at times. It allows you to come to a place where you can relate to where a person is and then find the tools that will help them move beyond that place. To become an encourager you have to be willing to actively instill courage in others through your actions.

- Create a wellspring of personal encouragement by developing tools that lift you up and motivate you. Make an encouragement CD or a segment in your iPod of songs that encourage your heart. Set aside a location where you can recharge and refocus. Keep a folder filled with poems, sayings and other words of encouragement. It is important to have a full encouragement tank of your own if you are going to pour it out on others.

· Be persistent and consistent with encouragement. Finding the positive in things may not come naturally, but optimism is the foundation for encouragement. You have to be determined to step up every day and look for the good, the positive and the uplifting in the life of your husband if you want those to flourish in his life .

Wives are called to lift up a husband · be a helpmeet that helps him meet up with the person that he has been designed to become. It is not about changing the man, but about adjusting the wife to find that inner man and then, with nurturing and love, to help him grow.

Seven Keys to Encouragement

1. Comfort - learning to console and give aid to those around you.

2. Motivate - being lifting up others to reach for the right actions.

3. Exhort - acting and speaking in ways that touch others in a positive way.

4. Counsel - providing comfort that allows others to find help and healing.

5. Inspire - emboldening the actions and attitudes of others.

6. Advise - admonishing with words and ideas that provide hope.

7. Console - standing alongside others giving aid and support.

The world pours out discouragement on my husband. I may never stop that bombardment, but I can still provide some comfort and a safe harbor in the storms. By learning to make encouragement a natural part of my day, I make it a natural part of our relationship.

My ability to encourage others came with the original package. I have heard rumors that I even encouraged the doctor after he delivered me, but those stories may be exaggerated a bit for effect. It has always felt right to lift up those around me, but I have not always succeeded in my efforts.

"Words cut deeper than any blade that exists on earth. Before you wield the blade of your words, be wary of their mark."

Secret 2

Sarcasm Disguised as Humor is NOT Always Funny

I grew up in a home that encouraged and supported my journey, but it also had a deep, dark, and dangerous secret. Every day, you could hear words that would talk down to others or to self - but it was always in a joking manner. We called it sarcasm and we wore it like a badge of honor.

It was utilized to make others laugh and for our own enjoyment. Everything would be fair game, and usually the contestant not paying attention quickly became the butt of most of the comments. It could be brutal business around our house.

My sarcastic wit - as I preferred to call it - could be annoying to others. It was only after I started having children of my own that I discovered those words I had been throwing around with sadistic humor could also be hurtful even to the people that I loved the most.

"You are no better off than some careless maniac shooting flaming arrows when you choose to say words that deceive and then say you were only joking."
- from Proverbs 26:18 - 19

Our firearms were secured in a gun safe to keep anyone from accidently injuring someone else, but I was recklessly shooting at the hopes and dreams of people with the words I let spill from my mouth.

Changing a habit formed over a lifetime takes persistence. I had to work at killing the sarcasm so that I could protect the innocent (and even the not so innocent) from the flaming arrows that I had spit out of my mouth. Years of practice have calmed my speech patterns, but there are still those moments when I find myself slipping back into the sarcasm realm - usually for the sake of humor.

Breaking a Word Habit

- Remember the old saying "if you are not able to say something nice then you should not say anything at all?" Creating a new way of talking may have to start with a few days of not talking at all.

- Start right now. Putting off the changes until tomorrow simply means you will never get around to changing that thing you want to change. Make this moment the beginning of a new way to talk.

- Ask for help and understanding. Take time to turn your words over to God each morning. Turn His words into your prayers. There are plenty of verses that you can choose to help you grow to understand the important and true value behind guarding your words.

· Think before you speak. It is possible, but not easy. There have been many comments I realized might be taken in the wrong way by someone · but could be oh, so funny for the rest of us. Slowing down to think about the words helped me make the better choice · the one that made healing more important than a laugh.

· Remember that words released can never be brought back. They go away and search out their target. Negative words will drain the energy and life of the people that they hit, and not even an apology or saying, "I was just joking," will be enough to push that power back into containment.

Most words are allowed to roam free with little regulation. The mouth opens up and pours out onto whatever happens to be close · and hits whoever might be least expecting it. The only time words might have any thought will be after they have done their damage and I am trying to fix the slashing those words provided.

Laughter makes for great medicine unless that laughter comes at the expense of another. Sarcastic comments to my husband or about my husband will tear down his strong shelters (or at least tear at them). I have to value each word I let loose if I want the words I share to build up.

"Do what you know to do - it may not make the rest of the world support or encourage your journey - but it will make the inevitable rug pulling, slapping in the face or diss a little easier to take.

It's not about what others see or think or do - it is about the choices that I make right now. Right now, I choose to do what I know to do and the rest will just have to fall to the side."

Secret 3
It is NOT about the Husband

My habits from growing up carried over into my first few years of marriage. I had my way of doing the dishes, the laundry and the cooking. My attitude towards the way my husband wanted to do things was that if he did it, he could do it that way. As long as the job fell on my shoulders I intended to do it the way I wanted and let the consequences fall where they may.

I prayed often for God to change my husband and help him to accept the things the way I did them. That translated in MY language as God doing whatever it took to get things moving in the directions I wanted. It was all about me. The number of nights I laid in bed wondering where God was and how He could be too busy to fix my husband are beyond measure. I talked to God, cried to God, whined to God and when that did not seem to work I started in on my husband. The results were a deeper hole, a bigger mess and more of the same. It was a vicious cycle that left me exhausted and fed up with the whole situation.

"God, fix my husband so that things get better." It was a last ditch plea to get the help I needed. The answer came to me from John 21:22 where Jesus and Peter are talking about how Peter will suffer at death and Peter wants to know what will happen with John.

I heard, "you let Me worry about him and you do what you know to do."

Apparently God agreed that it was all about me. He just had a different take on how that would work out in my life. The changes did not need to come from my husband. I needed to change what I was doing and focus on the things that God had called me to do.

Recognizing it IS all About Me

· Make God a priority. Putting God first in your day, in your walk and in your life will build a foundation that makes everything that comes next a little sounder.

· Plan ahead. Create a schedule that includes all appointments and events. Set up a menu that works with that schedule. Use the two to coordinate your days, allot time and even create a shopping list. A map helps in any journey, so map out a course for getting your life on track.

· Focus on what you need to be doing. I have discovered that if I spend my time and energy doing those things I know I should be doing then I have a lot less time to worry or complain about what I think my husband should be doing.

· Let go of the excuses. There will always be a reason to not be the wife that you know to be. You can blame your own upbringing, his upbringing, or the way he looked at you when you asked him to get take out for dinner. No matter what comes up, it is your choice to act on those issues or do what you have already determined needs to be done. Only YOU can make that choice so YOU hold the key.

· Give up the expectations. Your husband will never meet your needs. Accept that one point and the rest will be easier. We are not designed to be fulfilled by another person. That is a throne left for God to occupy. Look to God to be your answer.

Baby Steps to Big Changes

1. Make a list of the things that you want to accomplish – goals.

2. Make a list of how you will accomplish each of these things – objectives.

3. Write out the objectives in the form of a positive statement (I will write 500 words of fiction. I will send time with my family. I will send a note or card to a friend).

4. Estimate the amount of time that you think it will take each day to accomplish each task on your to do list and then total up the amount. Try to keep the time down to around 12 to 14 hours (this must include work time as well). You need to plan ample time for rest.

5. Create a chart on excel or publisher (or with a ruler and blank paper) with a block for each day of the week and a line for each to do item.

6. Pray over the list and make any changes or adjustments that will help you find your balance.

7. Start now to make a life of change

A sure sign of insanity is said to be the act of doing the same thing over and over again and expecting different results. Hitting my head up against the brick walls of my marriage gave me a headache, but did little more than that. I had to change the way I dealt with those issues that were blocking my progress by looking in the mirror. The change started in me.

"For real change to occur, I have to admit that I am the one with the problem. The first step to recovery is to admit that there is something to recover from at all. Until I face the issues, with a sincere heart, I will continue to deflect it all to the people, things and situations around me."

Secret 4
Acknowledge the Issues ~ Yours and His

I did not always like my husband during the first part of our marriage. There were days when he seemed so selfish and self-serving that I had no desire to be around him. I would stay up late hoping he would go to sleep so that I did not have to talk to him or I would hope that he would go spend time with friends so that I did not have to spend time with him.

Telling him anything scared me at times. His reactions overwhelmed me. The depths of his negativity threatened to capsize my boat of rainbows. It was not a pretty sight, even on those good days.

"The first step is admitting there is a problem." I had heard those words more times than I could count, but they finally struck home. We had issues and until those issues could be faced there would be no way the relationship could heal and mature in the manner it was designed to happen.

Discovering and Acknowledging the Issues

· Look in the mirror FIRST. I had to make a laundry list of those things I had wrong in my own life. The hurts, habits and hang-ups that drove my bad decisions and procrastination had to be exposed to the light. I wanted him to change, but I found that many of the things that bothered me about him stemmed from my own struggles.

- Take the necessary steps to make a difference. Not all of my laundry list could be washed clean overnight. Some of the habits I had been perfecting for decades. I had to consistently make choices that would replace my bad habits with new actions that would carry me in the right direction. After I started down that path, I had to work on making my consistency consistent. Every turn brought along a new test or burden that needed to be addressed. Each step forward brought me one step closer to my destination.

- Draw the line. Everyone has their limits. Know what yours are before they are upon you. I expressed my limits in no uncertain terms to my husband and to friends that I trusted. I also included the repercussions that would occur if those lines were drawn. It gave me comfort to know that I had a plan and I had people that would back up that plan. It created outside of "the moment," which left it reasoned and well thought out.

- Stand firm. Follow through with your plans. Continue pursuing your changes, but also be bold in holding the line. Consequences must be carried out if they are ever to hold value to those around you (parents would be wise to learn this method as well – and the sooner the better).

· Let it go. The past must be left behind or it will send you weaving all over the road. Healing for life starts with a heart that focuses on the potential of tomorrow and not the hurts of yesterday. Allow change to become a reality by choosing to see the possibilities and reaching for those · ALWAYS with the lines firmly in place.

· Be willing to change. It is not just about changing my actions and behaviors, but also my expectations. I review my lists as I grow and as the people around me begin their own growth process.

Pain should not be ignored. The mind, heart and body all use pain to show that a problem exists. I have to acknowledge the pain, recognize the source and then begin to map a path for healing.

Problems will continue to hold control and drag me into the darkness unless I take the steps to expose the issues to the light.

"I can see your actions, but I can never calculate into those actions the heart that drives them. Therefore, I can never judge your actions.

I must choose to love you for the heart that I cannot see and not for the actions that I can see."

Secret 5
You Will NEVER Change Him

It was all his fault. He had not even made an attempt to change - despite my eagerness to show him the areas that needed the most help. I pushed and prodded and poked and he still stayed him - what was he thinking?

I took my requests to God. "Make him a better husband, a better father and a better person." I continued my bible reading and again came across a story of Peter and Jesus. The one where Jesus tells Peter how he is going to die and Peter wants to know about John in John 21: 21 - 23. I read "you let me worry about him and you worry about you." (I keep being dragged back to that one).

That was not what I wanted to hear. I cried, I whined and I think I may have screamed a little over the next several months and years - all at God. My husband needed fixing and I expected God to do what needed to be done. I had to have read the words wrong in John.

I continued to poke and prod and nag and the stalemate continued as well. Something would have to change for anything to change.

I had my own Damascus moment coming home from the bank one day. My husband had a melt down and I had taken yet another moment point out the shortcomings of my spouse to my spouse. "Let me worry about him. "The words felt audible, but I knew they were only in my heart. The thought of ignoring them crossed my mind, but I chose to listen. Sometimes all the difference in the world begins with one choice.

"I should not have spoken to you that way. I am sorry." That was all that I offered. I left the rest of it in His hands, and it took me a few days to heal the cut on my lip from where I had to bite it on the trip home. A few days later, my husband went back to the bank on his own and apologized to the teller for his actions.

Who knew that God could do so much if a nagging wife would just get out of the way?

That was the moment that I gave up trying to change my husband. I still struggle at times, when my husband throws a temper tantrum (just like our youngest son) because he did not get his way, I want to point it out and call him a baby. Verbalizing that does not help the situation though. I have tried it. It usually makes matters worse because the youngest child then begins to chant "Daddy is a baby" from the backseat.

I work harder to give it over to God and to let Him worry about JOHN.

Top Tips for Getting out of the Way

- Learn to speak words that will clear the path for your husband to grow. Never, never, never condemn. The negative words of a wife are more powerful than anything else that a man encounters. Harsh words cut to the heart and are never spoken from a place of love. I learned first-hand how powerful a harsh word, spoken in anger, can be in the life of my husband. He has not forgotten, and the years of positive words since that one outburst have not managed to heal that wound.

– Pay attention to the beam and not the speck. The more I began to look at the struggles of my own life, the smaller his issues became. Even things that were BIG issues did not get me upset. I realized that he was not my responsibility, and that realization cleared the way for me to let go of a need to control him and his actions.

– Find some accountability. Join a group, or start up a group that will help you stay on task when it comes to dealing with a husband. I have been part of mom groups, women groups and online studies - and they have all made me face my own actions each day so that I continue to get better at staying out of his. *#1 Rule – NO HUSBAND BASHING.*

– Make prayer for his blessing a priority for your day. I quit praying for God to change my husband into what I wanted for several reasons. 1.) I knew that what God has planned is ALWAYS better than what I have planned. 2.) I struggled to understand my true wants for my husband so my requests had been changing. 3.) I often ended up doing more complaining than praying. My prayers shifted to a supporting role. "God, help me to be the wife my husband needs to become the man I know he is already in his heart."

- Listen to what your husband has to say. This was (and still often is) the toughest part for me to learn about getting out of his way. I get annoyed that I have to listen to his complaints about the way I do the laundry or make the bed or whatever is going to be suggested. But - and this is a MASSIVE one - the more I listen to him the less he tells me to change. By hearing his words, he is not compelled to point out every fault. And listening to him has opened up opportunities for us to talk and he then listens to me.

I continue to grow in my understanding of what it means to let God "worry about John." It is not easy and some days it seems impossible. But I keep P.U.S.H.ing (*Pray Until Something Happens*) and the more that I do that, the closer I get to where I am the helpmeet of my husband instead of a hindrance.

"IF is half of life and spending all the time in the if half means you never experience the fullness of life that God desires for you."

Secret 6
Whining Makes Things Worse

"That is NOT fair." Having multiple children means I hear this at least once a day. They are kids, so it is to be expected. The trouble comes when I am the one telling God that it is not fair and He comes back with the same line I use. "Life is not fair."

It is not about FAIR. It is about me doing what I know to do - and that is all that is it about.

The physical person in me demands her own way. She shouts and complains to every ear until she gets her way. The path she leaves behind reveals the destruction that her words and actions have caused. And then she looks around and realizes that standing there alone was not what she really wanted and she repeats the same process hoping that the end results will get better.

I had to get beyond the physical me, and it was a long battle that still has skirmishes that pop up now and then.

My change started with Proverbs. "A nagging woman (read that as a woman that complains A LOT) is as bad as a dripping roof" (from Proverbs 27:15).

A few years ago my son left a rock out under the overhang of our roof. By the spring, half of that rock had been eroded away because of the drips that

[29]

landed on it from the rain. The words from Proverbs let me see that my words had the same effect on the spirit, heart and soul of those people that had to endure them when I tossed them around recklessly.

Finding Ways to Get Past the Whine

1. Keep your mouth shut. Not talking will always be the easiest way to avoid complaining about an issue. Keep in mind that I am a talker by nature. I had to allow God to do a work in me to get me to a place where keeping my mouth shut was the first action of choice.

2. Listen to the words you are about to say. Slow down your response time long enough to hear the words before you release them. I have always felt like any quiet needed to be filled with words (and I would be more than willing to provide all the words if necessary). It takes effort for me to allow silence, but silence is the only place that I can hear the words. I allow the quiet and then I can determine if my words are a help or a hindrance.

3. Focus on what you are doing. There will be far less to complain about if you are only looking at the things you know you need to do. Worrying about what others should or should not be doing will only get in the way of your own lists. Worry will also steal your energy and your time along with that focus. I used to spend so much time thinking about ways that

my husband could be different that I missed my own opportunities to pursue my path. I had to choose to take my eyes off of his steps so that I could see my own direction.

4. Accept that things are not fair. I have determined that I do not want fair. Fair means that I get what I deserve, and do any of us REALLY want that? I live beyond fair and because of that location I am expected to do things in a way that is beyond fair. Sometimes that means that I have to sweep the floor that I just swept even if I did not get the crumbs under there. Other times it means that someone else will take the burden of my sins so that I can live free.

5. Recognize the whine. It usually starts with "I" and may also include a "but" or two. We had a group of women that used to meet every week. We all were presented with cards that had one letter on them. We called them the "I" card. Anytime one of us started down the whining path with the "I" statements, someone would hold up one of the cards. It was a reminder that when I am the focus, God is not.

Nothing good comes from whining. You end up in the corner alone or worse (just ask my kids). People may give in for a time just to keep you from whining, but they will leave in the end. No one wants to be around the constant complaints and negativities.

Get beyond the whining and complaining and start living for the joy.

"Choosing to focus on my own journey will keep me from getting in the way of your journey. Besides, I have enough to contend with without trying to keep the world spinning."

Secret 7
Doing what you know to do makes way for him to do what he needs to do

The life of a home schooling, work from home, mother of scouts/drama/choir kids seems to never slow down. Trying to push my husband along on this never-ending journey only adds to my frustration and exhaustion.

I have been known to ignore the dishes in the sink out of protest to him not doing what I felt like he should be doing. The next morning I would wake up to . . . even more dirty dishes. It seems that if left unattended those nasty little things managed to multiply like rabbits.

I have been known to intentionally not wake him for church because "I am not his mother" only to act shocked when we are unable to get up and get ready on time. I spent the day annoyed at him because he was annoyed at me and in the end all I had to show for it was tight muscles and little sleep.

There are plenty of things that I need to do every day. Making my husband do or be whatever it is that I have determined should never be one of them. The hours of the day are not plentiful enough to make that one task a reality.

Good days have been known to happen also.

There was this one day when I got up and got started, was not hindered by my husband sleeping in, kept my eye on the prize and got everything I needed to get done marked off my to do list. Maybe it has been more than one, but not by much.

The difference between my good day and my bad day lies in where I look. Keeping my eyes on my husband and what I think HE needs to be doing often lands me in a ditch. I stay in the game when my eye is on the ball in my court.

Staying focused when others are distracted can be tough. Most days I would prefer the easy way.

Tips for Doing My Thing When He is Not

1. Stop making to-do lists for him. There was a time when I made out a chore list that included things to do for everyone in the family. I even asked my husband which of the chores he would want to do. Every time I went to the list to make my plan for the day I had to be reminded of what he had chosen and then I began the process of fretting over whether it would get done (and usually topped the fretting with some nagging). Now, the chores are listed that have to be done, but I never put his name down next to one.

2. Stop comparing what he does with what you do - there will never be balance. Marriage (and life in general) is not about balance. I get more tasks accomplished when I am thinking about accomplishing tasks and not about what someone

else maybe doing better, faster or instead of what I think they should be doing.

3. Stop listening to the world. So many relationships (chores, work, and choices) are determined by the requirements and expectations of the world. The things of the Spirit will always confound even the wisest of the world. Some things are better handled by me than by my husband because of our personalities - I LOVE do it yourself projects and I am pretty sure they make him sick to his stomach. The sooner I quit adhering to the world order, the sooner we can find our own order to the way things need to work and happen.

4. Stop listening to your friends and family. The people that are closest to you will often have the hardest time being impartial. Even if your husband is in the right about a situation (and before you throw the book across the room I am NOT saying that he is right) they will side with you. Turn to people that you trust to be honest or just turn to the One that designed marriage in the first place.

5. Stop complaining about him, his actions or his inactions. The more that you focus in on his negatives, the brighter the light will be on those negatives. Fall back to the old standard of "if you cannot say anything nice then keep your mouth shut." Avoid even thinking those negatives. Keep

your eyes on your own prize (and your mouth shut) if you can do nothing else.

My husband will do what my husband will do. I have no control over the grown man and many years and much energy have been wasted proving that point. Letting go of the need to make him into what I want has opened a door to begin allowing God to mold him into what He wants.

"My course may not yet be settled, but my destination is firm. That fact renews a boldness in me that I had almost forgotten existed."

Secret 8
A relationship with God is a vital part of a relationship with your husband

It was important to me that God make my husband a great partner. I wanted the white knight, prince charming, superman that I had pieced together in my memories, dreams and my diary. Enough prayer and foot stomping would certainly make that a reality.

We changed churches early in our marriage to give my husband a chance to work with the youth drama at that new home. I discovered bible studies for the first time. I am sure they had always existed, but I had never known they were around. Besides, high school and college did not make me long for MORE study time.

One particular study came at the perfect time (and it always amazes me how God works that out). I devoured it and soon went searching for more. By the end of the year, I was doing a study in the morning before the kids were up, two during the mid-afternoon nap, and then one at night after they were asleep.

I loved getting to know the Word in a deeper, more personal way.

This journey also led me to a surprising realization. God did not promise me a perfect man. He promised me a help-meet that would walk with me (and sometimes carry me) into the purpose that God had designed for my life.

I spent more time with God. Each revelation brought me closer to who I am designed to be for Him and in Him. Each step closer to the me that God created made me a better me. The better the me, the easier it became on the people around me to become the person that God designed. We are now growing and learning together all because I made the choice to put my focus on God and not on the man in my life.

Building a Relationship with God

- Spend time in the Word. Nothing gives you confidence in your stand like a full understanding of the foundation. Take bible study classes. Follow study groups and curriculum (at church, online or start them in your home). Make the Word more important than football, the television show, the movie or the girls' night out.

- Open the Bible and read the words for yourself. Church can support your relationship with God, but it will never be in a position to build that relationship. READ, READ, READ the Word for yourself on a daily basis. Take notes about what you are reading and how you feel about it. Write down questions that you might have about the reading. Invest in a concordance so you can look up words or similar verses to help you find clarity.

- Talk to God. Forget the prayers and just have a conversation. Tell him what is on your mind, what is in your heart or even what you did during the day. Become comfortable talking to God not with the religious words of prayers, but with the honest heart of a friend!

- Slow down. Take time during the day to breathe. Breathe in for a count of six, hold that breath, and then let it out for a count of twelve. Repeat the process ten times (or as many as you can). Let your mind focus on your breath and nothing else. Just breathe.

- Listen to God. In the quiet of the moment, after you have slowed down to breathe, let the next few moments be the peace and calm of the Holy Spirit pouring into your heart and mind. Look for His words in the wind, the distant traffic or just the warmth of the sun on your face. He is talking to you all the time but you have to slow down, breathe and listen to what He is trying to say.

It has taken almost two decades to mold my husband into the man of my dreams, and most of it happened as I stopped working on him and focused on changing my own life. Who I am will cause me to see others in a new light. Becoming the me that God has designed makes it possible for my husband to make his own journey of discovery.

Getting to this place has not been easy, and it has usually been uncomfortable, but it has always been simple. All I have to do is focus my attention on loving God and loving others, and He can manage the rest.

The perfect husband may seem like a myth or an impossible dream. The reality is that as you become the better wife, mother, friend and person you will see the man you have in your life is growing into the one you know him to be in his heart.

About the Author

Facebook: theKathrynCLang
Twitter: @kathrynclang

Kathryn offers a phrase of hope in order to shine the Light on the moment. She works through her columns, articles, books and workshops. Her personal hope is that every person who encounters her words will feel as if those words were written (or spoken) just for her or him.

"In my fiction, I tell a story that provides an uplifting message entrenched in hope. In my non-fiction and columns, I offer words that will point to hope. In my talks, I tell stories that inspire hope. Helping others discover their path to hope is my focus.

I write to a woman that is trying to walk the tightrope of family, work and God – and keep them all in the right balance. She has a sense of humor, enjoys a little snark now and then, and references movies and songs in her every day speech. She plays with words and enjoys being around others that can keep up. She has a solid relationship with God, but hungers to go deeper. She is not afraid of faith in her own life or in the lives of those she encounters. She lives a life reaching for the rainbow."

Take a moment to visit www.kathrynlang.com to read more. You can also contact Kathryn to speak at your next event or conference by emailing her at kathrynlang@kathrynlang.com.

If you enjoyed what you read, please take a moment to visit the website where you purchased the book or your favorite book site and share a review.

Read more from Kathryn C. Lang

Blogs:
www.proverbs31life.com
www.kathrynclang.com

Books:
Practical Proverbs
Building Blocks to Writing Success
Place in Purpose
Reflections – Vol 1, Vol 2, Vol 3, Vol 4

Novels:
RUN
WATCH

Column:
Reflections from the Front Porch, *The Lakeside Post,*
Guntersville, Alabama.

Made in the USA
Middletown, DE
23 December 2021